P9-DNN-414

The MAYFLOWER COMPACT

By Kristen Rajczak

Gareth Stevens
Publishing

Please visit our website, www.garethstevens.com. For a free color catalog of all our high-quality books, call toll free 1-800-542-2595 or fax 1-877-542-2596.

Library of Congress Cataloging-in-Publication Data

Rajczak, Kristen.
The Mayflower Compact / by Kristen Rajczak.
  p. cm. — (Documents that shaped America)
Includes index.
ISBN 978-1-4339-9006-9 (pbk.)
ISBN 978-1-4339-9007-6 (6-pack)
ISBN 978-1-4339-9005-2 (library binding)
1. Mayflower Compact—(1620)—Juvenile literature. 2. Mayflower (Ship)—Juvenile literature. 3. Pilgrims (New Plymouth Colony)—Juvenile literature. I. Rajczak, Kristen. II. Title.
F68.R35 2014
 974.4'82—d23

First Edition

Published in 2014 by
Gareth Stevens Publishing
111 East 14th Street, Suite 349
New York, NY 10003

Copyright © 2014 Gareth Stevens Publishing

Designer: Sarah Liddell
Editor: Therese Shea

Photo credits: Cover, p. 1 SuperStock/SuperStock/Getty Images; p. 5 (Pilgrims) Lambert/Contributor/Hulton Fine Art Collection/Getty Images; p. 5 (Magna Carta) Henry Guttmann/Stringer/Hulton Archive/Getty Images; p. 6 Duncan Walker/E+/ Getty Images; pp. 7, 12 Archive Photos/Stringer/Archive Photos/Getty Images; pp. 8, 11 UniversalImagesGroup/Contributor/Universal Images Group/Getty Images; p. 9 George Eastman House/Contributor/Archive Photos/Getty Images; p. 10 photo courtesy of Wikimedia Commons, 17th-century-merchantman.jpg; p. 13 Time Life Pictures/Contributor/Time & Life Pictures/Getty Images; p. 14 photo courtesy of Wikimedia Commons, VirginiaCompanyofLondonSeal-1606-1624.png; p. 15 MPI/Stringer/ Archive Photos/Getty Images; p. 16 photo courtesy of Wikimedia Commons, Mayflower Compact Bradford.jpg; p. 17 photo courtesy of Wikimedia Commons, The Mayflower Compact 1620 cph.3g07155.jpg; p. 18 Three Lions/Stringer/Hulton Archive/ Getty Images; p. 19 photo courtesy of Wikimedia Commons, Landing of the Pilgrims by Corné - circa 1805.jpg; pp. 20, 23 Kean Collection/Staff/Archive Photos/Getty Images; p. 21 PhotoQuest/Contributor/Archive Photos/Getty Images; p. 22 John Nordell/ Contributor/Getty Images; p. 25 photo courtesy of Wikimedia Commons, Plymouth Colony map.svg; p. 27 DEA/M. SEEMULLER/Contributor/De Agostini/Getty Images; p. 27 Frederic Lewis/Staff/Getty Images; p. 28 photo courtesy of Wikimedia Commons, Us declaration independence.jpg; p. 29 photo courtesy of WIkimedia Commons, Constitution of the United States, page 1.jpg.

Printed in the United States of America

CPSIA compliance information: Batch #CS13GS: For further information contact Gareth Stevens, New York, New York at 1-800-542-2595.

CONTENTS

Words in the glossary appear in **bold** type the first time they are used in the text.

BEGINNINGS

Despite fierce storms and rough seas, 102 men, women, and children on a ship called the *Mayflower* sailed safely into Cape Cod, Massachusetts, in November 1620. Known today as Pilgrims, they were weary from enduring 2 months of tossing waves and seasickness. No doubt they were anxious about starting a new life so far from the one they had known in Europe. Some of the group had escaped years of religious **persecution**.

Before even setting foot on land, the group agreed to the Mayflower Compact, the first written framework of government established in the New World. Though only about 200 words long, this **document** helped set the tone for future governments in the British colonies—and eventually in the United States.

It's a Fact!

The word "pilgrim" can mean anyone who takes a long journey, commonly for religious reasons. The group who landed at Cape Cod in 1620 weren't called Pilgrims until the early 1800s.

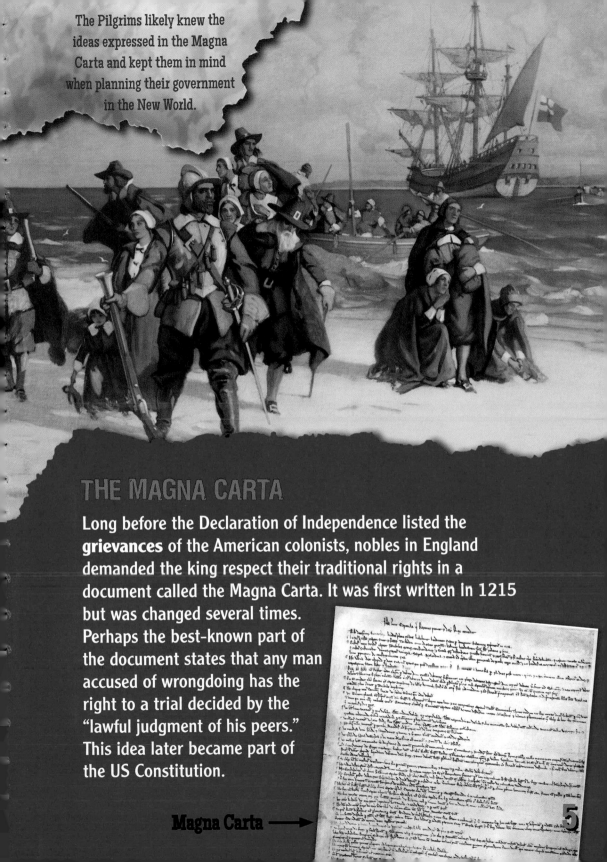

The Pilgrims likely knew the ideas expressed in the Magna Carta and kept them in mind when planning their government in the New World.

THE MAGNA CARTA

Long before the Declaration of Independence listed the **grievances** of the American colonists, nobles in England demanded the king respect their traditional rights in a document called the Magna Carta. It was first written in 1215 but was changed several times. Perhaps the best-known part of the document states that any man accused of wrongdoing has the right to a trial decided by the "lawful judgment of his peers." This idea later became part of the US Constitution.

Magna Carta ⟶

5

During the 1600s, it was illegal in England to belong to any church other than the Church of England. **Dissenters** were fined and could even be thrown in jail. Tired of this treatment, a group called the Separatists left England in 1608 and settled in the Netherlands.

Though the Separatists stayed in the city of Leiden for more than 10 years, they weren't content in the Netherlands. They could practice their faith openly, but they found little work and didn't have much money. In addition, their children seemed to be forgetting their English **heritage**. There were also concerns about a war between the Dutch and the Spanish. By 1620, the Separatists were ready to leave. They decided to go to the British colonies.

King Henry VIII

It's a Fact!

Though the Separatists left England, they remained loyal to the British king.

6

In this image, the Separatists leave the Netherlands, praying for a better life in the British colonies in America.

THE CHURCH OF ENGLAND

After a disagreement with the pope, King Henry VIII turned against the Roman Catholic Church. He established a new church called the Church of England in 1534 and made himself its leader. After a time, many people in England became unhappy with the new church. A group called the Puritans wanted changes made. Others, called Separatists, wanted to separate from the Church of England and form new churches. Both the Separatists and Puritans faced persecution in England.

7

For the money and supplies they needed for the journey, the Separatists turned to the Virginia Company of London, a group of investors. In exchange, the Separatists agreed to send natural resources such as wood and furs from the colonies to the business for 7 years. Their land and homes would belong to the Virginia Company during that period, too.

The group living in the Netherlands planned to establish a farming community in the northern part of the Virginia Colony, near present-day New York City. The Virginia Company granted the Separatists a legal document stating they had permission from the king for their settlement. This is called a charter or patent. The document was only meant for Virginia, however, which had far-reaching effects.

It's a Fact!

Some of the Pilgrims weren't Separatists. They were passengers who also wished to travel to America. The Separatists sometimes called these passengers "strangers."

JAMESTOWN, VIRGINIA

Established in 1607, the colony of Jamestown was the first successful British colony in North America. It was settled by the Virginia Company. By the time the Pilgrims left England, Jamestown was growing in population and prosperity. Tobacco crops were flourishing. The colonists had begun electing their own representatives to a colonial assembly headed by a royal governor. In addition, the first ship with slaves had arrived.

Native Americans greeted and aided the Jamestown colonists in establishing their new settlement.

ABOARD the MAYFLOWER

On September 6, 1620, the Pilgrims set sail on a ship provided by the Virginia Company. The *Mayflower* wasn't a passenger ship. Before carrying the Pilgrims, it had been transporting goods all around Europe. While the captain of the ship had warm, dry quarters, there weren't rooms for passengers to sleep in. So, for 66 days, the Pilgrims lived in the windowless lower deck where the *Mayflower* usually held its cargo.

Rough seas and the unwelcoming space made the journey aboard the *Mayflower* uncomfortable. The Pilgrims brought food such as bacon, biscuits, cabbage, and turnips—but they often felt too seasick to eat. Their vegetables ran out eventually, and they had to eat bowls of mush and oatmeal.

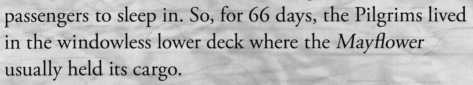

It's a Fact!

Pilgrims were left behind in England. There wasn't enough room on one ship for everyone.

The Pilgrims are rowed out to the *Mayflower* from a dock in England in 1620.

THE *SPEEDWELL*

The Separatists bought a small boat called the *Speedwell*. They wanted it for the journey across the ocean and as a fishing boat when they reached America. The *Speedwell* met the *Mayflower* and its passengers in Southampton, England. But when the two ships set out, the *Speedwell* leaked, forcing the group to turn back twice! By September, the *Speedwell* was left behind while the *Mayflower* continued on to the New World.

By November 1620, the *Mayflower* was nearing its destination. However, the winds weren't in the Pilgrims' favor. The ship had been driven much farther north than the group wanted to go. Instead of traveling to the Hudson River, the *Mayflower* had sailed into Cape Cod, near what is now Provincetown Harbor. The Pilgrims tried to continue around Cape Cod and then south, but storms made this impossible. The group decided that it was too late in the year to keep going, and they would try to land in Cape Cod Bay. This decision wasn't welcomed by all.

Many of the "strangers" who had joined the Separatists' party to the New World began to change their minds about the settlement. They threatened to leave.

Myles Standish

It's a Fact!

The Pilgrims brought a British soldier named Myles Standish to be their military leader. Standish later headed talks with Native American tribes, which sometimes led to fighting.

On the *Mayflower* voyage, the waves were so rough that one "stranger" was swept overboard and drowned.

A DANGEROUS JOURNEY

Traveling aboard a ship in the 1600s was much more dangerous than it is today. Seasickness was common, and other illnesses spread easily because quarters were usually cramped. The crew had to watch out for attack by other ships and even pirates! The *Mayflower* didn't meet any pirates, but it did experience another serious ocean danger—a major storm. Part of the ship was damaged, but luckily it could be fixed.

The Virginia Company's charter applied to the area of Virginia the Pilgrims had been trying to reach. When the group arrived in Cape Cod instead, the charter no longer legally bound them together. The Separatists and other passengers, members of the Church of England, didn't have a shared faith keeping them together, either. Tension began building. Some of the Pilgrims thought they should break away and work for themselves, instead of the Virginia Company. They freely shared this opinion aboard the *Mayflower*.

The Separatist leaders wanted a way to keep the passengers peacefully working together to survive. They began to write an agreement. Called the Mayflower Compact today, the document was written on board the ship for which it was named.

seal of the Virginia Company

It's a Fact!

The original Mayflower Compact has never been found.

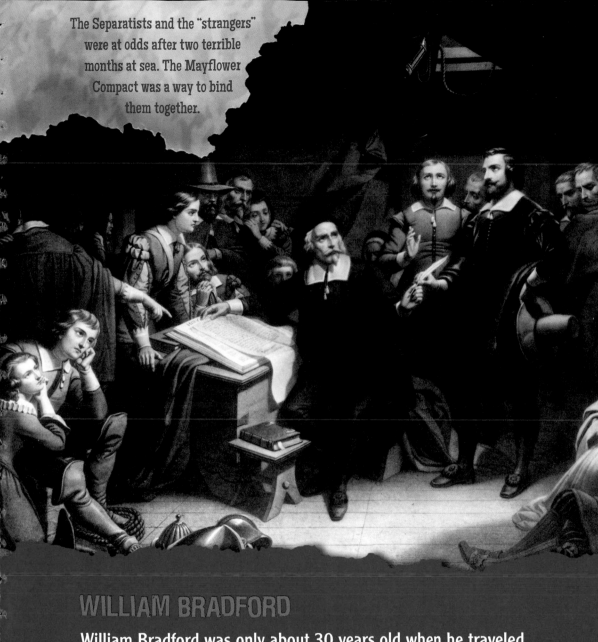

The Separatists and the "strangers" were at odds after two terrible months at sea. The Mayflower Compact was a way to bind them together.

WILLIAM BRADFORD

William Bradford was only about 30 years old when he traveled with the Pilgrims to North America. Despite his young age, he was an influential part of the group. He helped write the Mayflower Compact and was elected governor of the colony 31 times! Much of what historians know about the journey on the *Mayflower* and the early Pilgrims comes from Bradford's book *History of Plymouth Plantation, 1620–47*.

The
MAYFLOWER COMPACT

First, the Mayflower Compact established the signers were "Loyal Subjects" of King James. They promised that their voyage and the founding of the colony "in the northern Parts of Virginia" had been undertaken for the "Advancement of the Christian Faith" and to honor their "King and Country."

The signers formally bound themselves together into a group they called the "civil Body Politick" for their "better Ordering and Preservation." The Compact gave only a broad description of how a government should oversee the group but not what it would actually consist of. It said the signers pledged to "enact, constitute, and frame such just and equal laws, **ordinances**, acts, constitutions, and offices . . . for the general good of the colony."

RELIGIOUS COVENANT

The Mayflower Compact was based on the covenants made in the Separatist Church. A covenant is an agreement between people, though it's often used in religions to mean an agreement between God and man. The Separatists used both definitions of "covenant." They believed the document created an agreement not just between the passengers on the *Mayflower*, but also the passengers and God. In fact, this religious idea is stated directly in the document.

The Mayflower Compact was signed by 41 of the male passengers on November 11, 1620.

The Pilgrim leaders wanted to suppress the **mutinous** ideas of some *Mayflower* passengers. So, the Mayflower Compact ended with a promise that the signers would give "all due Submission and Obedience" to the colony.

The government immediately went into effect upon the signing, and the Pilgrims chose John Carver as their governor. It was the first occurrence of European self-governance in the colonies. Though elections weren't outlined in the document, the ideas behind the Mayflower Compact made this example of **democracy** possible. As the first settlers in this part of America, the Pilgrims paved the way for those who followed.

What the document didn't do was give the colonists legal rights to the land in New England. They needed to ask for another charter from England for their settlement.

It's a Fact!

John Carver didn't hold the office of governor long. He died in April 1621.

While there aren't any photographs of the *Mayflower* or the Pilgrims because photography hadn't been invented, many artists have painted their idea of the journey and arrival in Cape Cod.

OLD-STYLE CALENDAR

Though the Mayflower Compact says it was signed November 11, 1620, some sources report the date as November 21. England and the colonies used a different calendar than we do today. Their "Old Style" calendar was created around 46 BC. However, its years were about 11 minutes too long, so eventually the calendar year and solar year didn't agree. In 1752, the Gregorian calendar was put in place to correct this.

BUILDING the COLONY

After the Mayflower Compact was signed, the Pilgrims waited a few more weeks before they **disembarked**. They sent a group to find a suitable place to build their colony. The Pilgrim explorers chose the site of a Native American settlement that had been abandoned by the Wampanoag tribe. (Most members of the tribe had died of an illness brought to their community by European explorers.)

The site was ideal for the Pilgrims' needs. There was lots of water, and there were cleared fields ready for planting. Plus, it was on a hill, which would help them spot anyone who approached. The Pilgrims called the place Plimoth (now Plymouth). The Pilgrims sailed into Plymouth Harbor in December 1620, ready to make a new community there.

It's a Fact!

The Pilgrims soon met some Wampanoag and even signed a treaty with Massasoit, the leader of a tribe.

While Plymouth Rock isn't mentioned in any Pilgrims' accounts of their arrival at Plymouth, it has become part of the Pilgrim story through later records about the settlement.

SICKNESS AND DEATH

The first winter in Plymouth was cold and difficult. The Pilgrims continued to live on the ship while houses and other buildings were constructed on land. Their poor diets on the *Mayflower* left them weak. Cold wind and water blew all around them as they traveled from the ship to the shore while working on the settlement. Many Pilgrims fell ill—and about half of them died during that first winter.

The weary Pilgrims began living in Plymouth in March 1621. By then, enough homes had been built for them to leave the ship for good. The *Mayflower* returned to England the following month.

Over the next few years, many of those who had been left in England in 1620 because there was no room on the *Mayflower* came to Plymouth. The Pilgrims began to trade with nearby Native Americans and to farm and fish. They used the Mayflower Compact as the foundation of their government. Though the Separatists were a **minority**, the leaders of the colony were mostly from this group. Year after year, the adult men of the colony voted in elections, and the power remained with just a few settlers.

Mayflower II

It's a Fact!

At Plimoth Plantation in Plymouth, Massachusetts, visitors can see a full-scale copy, or replica, of the *Mayflower* called the Mayflower II.

THE SECOND CHARTER

The Pilgrims asked for and were granted a second charter in 1621, allowing them to stay in Plymouth legally. However, the charter was conditional. The settlement had to last 7 years in order to apply for a permanent charter. In 1629, the Pilgrims finally received another charter. It was called the Warwick Patent or Bradford Patent, after the Earl of Warwick who signed the charter and William Bradford to whom it was addressed.

Tisquantum, commonly known as Squanto today, was a Wampanoag who had lived in England. He helped the Pilgrims grow corn when they first settled at Plymouth.

A GROWING COMMUNITY

The Mayflower Compact allowed for the Plymouth Colony's needs to determine when laws should be made and when changes in government should happen. As more people came to live in Plymouth in the 1630s, small towns formed around the main settlement. People began to choose representatives to speak for them at colonial government meetings.

By this time, Plymouth wasn't the only settlement in New England. About 1,000 Puritans sailed from England in 1630. They settled the Massachusetts Bay Colony, including the cities of Salem and Boston.

In 1691, the Massachusetts Bay Colony was granted a new charter from England. It joined the Plymouth Colony to Massachusetts Bay under the British government. That meant the end of the Mayflower Compact's use.

It's a Fact!

By the 1640s, about 3,000 people lived in the Plymouth Colony.

MASSACHUSETTS BAY COLONY

The Puritans founded the Massachusetts Bay Colony with the wish to practice their religion freely. But an **omission** in their first English charter allowed for a significant move toward democracy in America. Instead of having to complete colony business in England, the charter allowed them to set up a government in the colonies. However, it wasn't wholly democratic: People who weren't part of their church couldn't vote.

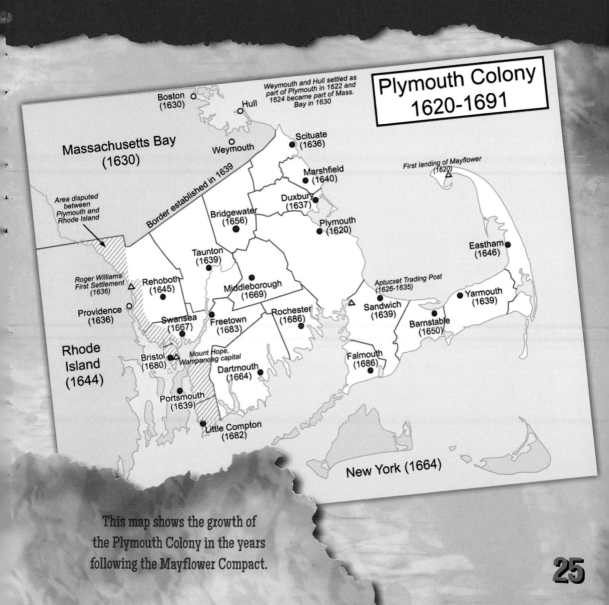

Boston (1630)

Hull

Weymouth and Hull settled as part of Plymouth in 1622 and 1624 became part of Mass. Bay in 1630

Plymouth Colony
1620-1691

Massachusetts Bay (1630)

Weymouth

Scituate (1636)

Marshfield (1640)

First landing of Mayflower (1620)

Area disputed between Plymouth and Rhode Island

Border established in 1639

Duxbury (1637)

Bridgewater (1656)

Plymouth (1620)

Eastham (1646)

Taunton (1639)

Roger Williams' First Settlement (1636)

Rehoboth (1645)

Middleborough (1669)

Aptucxet Trading Post (1626-1635)

Yarmouth (1639)

Providence (1636)

Swansea (1667)

Freetown (1683)

Rochester (1686)

Sandwich (1639)

Barnstable (1650)

Rhode Island (1644)

Bristol (1680)

Mount Hope, Wampanoag capital

Dartmouth (1664)

Falmouth (1686)

Portsmouth (1639)

Little Compton (1682)

New York (1664)

This map shows the growth of the Plymouth Colony in the years following the Mayflower Compact.

INTERPRETING the COMPACT

Though around 200 words, the Mayflower Compact's meaning has been **debated** for many years. Some look to the actions of the Pilgrims for clues about what the original writers meant.

Some historians interpret the Mayflower Compact to mean that the Pilgrims wanted to create a government based on equality—but that's not stated in the document. And Plymouth was generally ruled by a small group of **elite** settlers. However, it's also said that the Pilgrims' writing of the Mayflower Compact implies a belief in government created by the people (or at least the men of a community). This may be true, as all adult men could vote in elections and, later, the colonists chose representatives. Again, though, this isn't stated in the Mayflower Compact.

It's a Fact!

The original Mayflower Compact has been lost. The first copy historians found is in a **pamphlet** called *Mourt's Relation* from 1622.

President John Quincy Adams was related to John Alden, a passenger on the *Mayflower*. Alden is shown here with his wife.

PRESIDENTIAL WORDS

In 1802, President John Quincy Adams made a speech in which he stated the importance of the Mayflower Compact. He said it was the first modern example of a group of men acting as equals agreeing to create a community and government. While Adams also said it laid a foundation for the US Constitution, most historians believe the Mayflower Compact was a small step toward democracy but didn't directly influence the content of the Constitution.

John Quincy Adams

The Pilgrims were ahead of their time when they established their government under the Mayflower Compact, and they managed to reach their goal of keeping the community together. The characteristics of many modern democratic principles had taken hold in colonial America.

Have you ever read the Declaration of Independence? What about the US Constitution? These documents came more than 150 years after the Mayflower Compact. And while they may not closely resemble the Pilgrims' brief document, all three were written with a similar spirit: a group of people choosing to unite for the good of all. It's this spirit, as well as the seeds of democracy, that makes the Mayflower Compact one of the documents that shaped America.

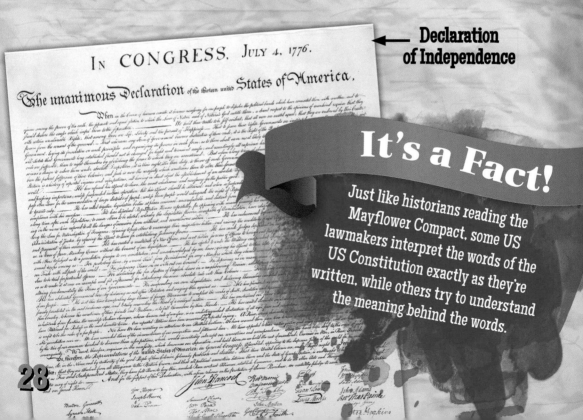

Declaration of Independence

IN CONGRESS. JULY 4, 1776.

The unanimous Declaration of the thirteen united States of America.

It's a Fact!

Just like historians reading the Mayflower Compact, some US lawmakers interpret the words of the US Constitution exactly as they're written, while others try to understand the meaning behind the words.

We the People *of the United States, in...*

Article. 1.

Section. 1. All legislative Powers herein granted shall be vested in a Congress of the United...

US Constitution

Historians aren't in agreement about the amount of influence the Mayflower Compact had on later US documents. What do you think?

THE PILGRIMS' JOURNEY

1608
The Separatists leave England to settle in the Netherlands.

DECEMBER 1620
The Plymouth settlement begins to be built.

1691
Plymouth and the Massachusetts Bay Colony combine.

SEPTEMBER 1620
The Pilgrims leave England aboard the *Mayflower*.

APRIL 1621
The *Mayflower* sails back to England.

NOVEMBER 1620
The *Mayflower* arrives in Cape Cod Bay. The Mayflower Compact is signed.

1629
Plymouth is granted another charter to settle in New England.

JULY 1620
The *Speedwell* and the *Mayflower* leave England together and turn back twice because of leaks in the *Speedwell*.

MARCH 1621
The Pilgrims leave the ship.

1622
The Mayflower Compact is published in *Mourt's Relation*.

GLOSSARY

debate: an argument or public discussion

democracy: the free and equal right of every person to participate in a government

disembark: to get off a ship or other vehicle

dissenter: someone who voices a difference of opinion, especially to someone in power

document: a formal piece of writing

elite: a higher social class

grievance: a formal complaint

heritage: something that comes from past members of a family or group

minority: people who are not part of the main group of a society

mutinous: refusing to obey an authority

omission: something that has been left out or not done

ordinance: a law or rule

pamphlet: a small book that gives information

persecution: making a group of people suffer cruel or unfair treatment

FOR MORE INFORMATION

BOOKS

Raum, Elizabeth. *The Mayflower Compact*. Chicago, IL: Heinemann Library, 2012.

Smith, Andrea P. *The Journey of the Mayflower*. New York, NY: PowerKids Press, 2012.

Wagner, Heather Lehr. *William Bradford*. New York, NY: Chelsea House Publishers, 2011.

WEBSITES

Ben's Guide to U.S. Government for Kids: Historical Documents
bensguide.gpo.gov/3-5/documents/index.html
Read about some important documents from US history.

Plimoth Plantation
www.plimoth.org/
Learn more about the history of Plimoth Plantation and how you can visit it today.

INDEX